The
Secret Shopper
Handbook

Tips for Retailers

Gail Cassidy

Printed in the United States of America, First Printing,

Tomlyn Publications
547 Shackamaxon Drive
Westfield, NJ 07090
http://www.coachability.com

gail@coachability.com

DEDICATION

To all of the hard-working retailers who want and need their businesses to succeed, I commend you for your intentions and your perserverence.

Having passion for your employees, passion for your customer, and passion for your company are what separate the great companies from the good ones. Businesses flourish by being able to attract and keep customers.

Happy employees impact customers and are the reasons cusomters return again and again. Having employees go the extra mile with customers separates your company from the competition, thus creating uniqueness. This is critical, and because you are reading this book, I know you truly care not only for your customers but also for your employees.

Congratulations!

Table of Contents

The Secret Shopper Handbook

Tips for Retailers

THE SECRET SHOPPER HANDBOOK

Dealing with people professionally on a daily basis can be a fun, exciting, and satisfying experience, but it is also one that can be filled with challenges and frustrations.

Products change. Times change. One thing, however, that does not change is human nature.

The two primary basics of human nature are as follows:

(1) **Everyone wants to be appreciated**. That is not to say that customers will appreciate you, but deep down, they want to be appreciated and/or accepted.

(2) **Nobody likes to be wrong**. We all are wrong on occasion, but we don't like to be. In your business, you deal with customers all day, and they may insist they are right, which means, of

course, that you or your company are wrong--
even though you know that is not so.

The saying "The customer is always right" is not
meant to be taken literally. The literal translation is
"The customer must be made to feel as if they are
right--even if they are not."

That is the challenge, and hopefully this booklet will
help address that challenge.

Keep in mind what is most important--without
customers you would not have your job and your
employer would not have his/her business.

Enjoy reading the tips. Highlight those you want to
keep in the forefront of your mind. Enjoy your
customers. Make each day fun.

Customers have unique ideas and individual
perspectives, and, with your guidance, your
experiences with them will provide you with the gift
of never-ending fond memories.

Best wishes,
Gail Cassidy

PHILOSOPHY

1.   See the invisible tattoo on every person's forehead that reads: "PLEASE MAKE ME FEEL IMPORTANT."

2.   Find at least one happening in each day to be grateful for.

3.   Look for positives in every customer.

4.   Recognize the specialness of diversity.

5.   Provide an atmosphere conducive to working, e.g. cleanliness, organization, lighting, safety, etc.

6.   Learn the Serenity Prayer: "God, grant me the serenity to accept the things I cannot change, courage to change the things I can and the wisdom to know the difference."

7.   "See" and/or "feel" your positive day before it begins via positive self talk.

8.   Be (or act) enthusiastic about everything you do. It's contagious; it carries over to the customers.

9.   Accept customers as they are, and then provide the atmosphere for them to make their purchases.

10.   Learn from every person you deal with.

11.   Ask yourself, "Does it really matter?"

12.   Being RIGHT does not always work, e.g.,
       Here lies the body of William Jay, who died maintaining his right of way. He was right, dead right as he sped along, but he's just as dead as if he were wrong.

13.   HAVE FUN!

ATTITUDE

14. Park your ego at the door; it hinders relationships with customers.

15. Give customers a reason to check their negative attitudes at the door also.

16. Know that customers "mirror" you. They reflect what they see, hear, and feel from you.

17. Show customers through your own example what fun having a great attitude is.

18. Be patient.

19. Positive attitudes at work are catching.

20. Show respect to get respect.

21. Know that attitude is a choice everyone makes every day.

22. Know that people cannot help what happens to them, but they are always in charge of their responses.

23. Remember, there is a pause between stimulus and response. Choose your response carefully.

24. Know that attitude is the steering mechanism of the brain. Body language can lead to attitude.

25. Practice changing your attitude by sitting or standing straight, with your head up, and a smile on your face. It does work!

26. Know that it is the attitude of our hearts and minds that shape who we are, how we live, and how we treat others.

27. Recognize your own specialness.

28. Success is feeling good about yourself every single day. That is attitude.

29. Understand that true power is knowing that you can control your attitude at all times.

HUMAN RELATIONS

30. Treat every customer as if he or she were your friend.

31. Never talk down to anyone.

32. Find what is special about every customer, when applicable.

33. **SMILE.** It warms a room.

34. Use tact when responding to a challenging customer. The rewards outweigh "being right."

35. Know that it is not okay for any customer to feel your negativity.

36. Be 100% fair at all times--no exceptions.

37. Keep in mind that perception is reality--yours and your customers.

38. Treat every person as you wish to be treated.

39. Understand that no one wants to be wrong.

40. Everyone desperately wants to feel special.

41. Remember that people gravitate toward things that are pleasurable and avoid things that are painful. Make dealing with your company pleasurable.

42. **LISTENING** is the greatest compliment.

43. Try to understand before being understood.

44. Show genuine appreciation to your customers.

45. Never embarrass a customer. Allow him/her to save face.

46. Use encouragement. Make an error seem easy to correct.

47. Don't be afraid to admit your mistakes. It will make you appear more human to customers.

48. Show respect for every customer's opinion.

49. Make **SINCERITY** your #1 priority.

COMMUNICATION

50.   Know that 55% of all messages comes from the body. Notice how you can tell your special someone is in a bad mood without any words being spoken. You can see the same in your customers as they can in you.

51.   Know that 38% of the message comes from the voice: inflection, intonation, pitch, speed, e.g., "I didn't say he stole the watch." Seven words = seven meanings.

52.   Know, you cannot **NOT** communicate.

53.   Recognize that we don't all see the same thing when looking at the same thing.

54.   Know also that we don't all hear the same things even when listening to the same words.

55.   Control your thoughts; your feelings come from your thoughts; therefore, you can also control your feelings! Choice is control.

56. Take responsibility for what you say and how you say it.

57. Listen for the message, yet know that body language can be interpreted as only a clue to the meaning of the message, e.g., arms crossed in front of chest could mean blocking you or could mean the person is actually cold or comfortable.

58. Learn to lead rather than to try and overcome resistance.

59. Communicate your enthusiasm through your body and voice.

60. "One who is too insistent on his own views, find few to agree with him." -Lao-Tze

61. Speak with a warm heart.

UNDERSTANDING

62. Know that a person with high self-esteem does not need to find fault with others. They find fault when they feel threatened, consciously or unconsciously.

63. Know that self-esteem is not noisy conceit. It is a quiet sense of self-respect, a feeling of self-worth. Conceit is whitewash to cover low self-esteem.

64. Remember, people have two basic needs: to know they are lovable and worthwhile.

65. Remember, it is the customer's feeling about being respected or not respected that affects how s/he will react.

66. Insight: Masks are worn to hide the "worthless me."

67. Low self-esteem is tied to impossible demands on the self.

68. An employee's own self-acceptance frees him or her to focus on the customer, unencumbered by inner needs.

69. The single most important ingredient in a supportive relationship is honesty.

70. Ask this: "If I were to treat my customers as I treat my children, how many customers would I have left?"

71. Avoid mixed messages. Be clear in your statements.

RESPECTFULNESS

72. Do not ever be disrespectful to a customer, nor should you tolerate disrespect.

73. Be consistent in following the rules, understanding that on occasion changes may have to be made.

74. Uncover and address, when possible, the reasons for the customer's dissatisfaction.

75. Focus, as often as possible, on what is right rather than what is wrong.

76. Set an example by turning any problem into a learning opportunity.

77. Approach dissatisfied customers with relaxed confidence.

78. Being a model for customers to follow provides them with a picture of what appropriate behavior looks like.

79. Respond thoughtfully to challenging and/or problem situations--avoid making judgments.

80. Know the steps in problem solving:
    o Define the problem
    o Locate the causes of the problem
    o Brainstorm solutions
    o Select the best one

81. Encourage customers to see beyond their own point of view.

82. Show lively enthusiasm!

83. Create an atmosphere of fun.

84. Make every customer feel important.

WHAT IS A CUSTOMER?

(Reprinted L.L. Bean, Inc.)

85. A customer is the most important person ever in this company--in person or by mail.

86. A customer is not dependent on us; we are dependent on him.

87. A customer is not an interruption of our work; he is the purpose of it.

88. We are not doing a favor by servicing him; he is doing us a favor by giving us the opportunity to do so.

89. A customer is not someone to argue or match wits with. Nobody ever won an argument with a customer.

90. A customer is a person who brings us his wants. It is our job to handle them profitably to him and to ourselves.

TEN WAYS TO APPRECIATE CUSTOMERS

(Reprint: General Motors Corporation)

Obey the golden rule ("Do unto others as you would have them do unto you").

91. Use praise (Be generous and others will respond in a positive manner).

92. Be sincere (A customer's trust depends on your sincerity).

93. Use the customer's name (Everyone enjoys being recognized).

94. Be a friend (It takes one to know one).

95. Smile (It's the best way to hear what the customer is saying).

96. Listen (It's the shortest distance between two people).

97. Give (The customer will see and appreciate the value received).

98. Think "you" instead of "I," (Consciously use the word and always retain your sense of humor).

99. Care for the customer (Actions speak louder than words).

CUSTOMERS: WHAT THEY WANT FROM BUSINESSES

(reprint: General Motors)

- Cleanliness
- To feel important
- Sincerity
- Honesty and Integrity
- Trust
- Eye-Pleasing Environment

TO HELP CUSTOMERS, BUSINESSES NEED TO

(reprint: General Motors)

- Believe in our product
- Be convinced of their needs
- Avoid showing anger

- Remain courteous

- Remember they want benefits
- Ask questions
- Give them full attention
- Say thank you

TIPS FOR EMPLOYERS

- Validate your employees on a regular basis, not just during a once-a-year review.

- Tell employees specifically what you like about what they are doing. They will work harder to earn that recognition again in the future.

- Encourage employees to strive for excellence. "We are what we repeatedly do. Excellence, then, is not an act but a habit." -Aristotle.

- Encourage employees to align their goals with their values. Conflict arises when the two are in conflict.

- Expect the best from your staff. People live up to expectations.

- Always abide by the golden rule: "Do unto others as you would have them do unto you."

- Involve as many employees as you can in company activities. Those who participant feel more a part of the "family."

- Always always be fair.

- Avoid being judgmental.

- Treat your staff to bagels one morning a week. Let them know you care.

- Encourage employees to use their powers of observation and logic. Successful employees see details & discover principles that others do not.

- Encourage and enable employees to continually grow. Complacency breeds stagnation.

- Make your business an inviting place to work.

- Make your employees proud to be a part of your "family."

TIPS FOR ALL EMPLOYEES

- Work towards feeling good about yourself. It is man's highest goal.

- Always do what you feel is right or true.

- Your actions reveal your values.

- Your thought is the most powerful force in your universe. "Nothing is either good or bad but thinking makes it so." -Shakespeare.

- Whatever you dwell on expands.

- Work toward goals that cause you to feel a sense of mastery.

- Write a list of everything you have accomplished or have been recognized for in your life. Add to it whenever you think of something new. Read it when the going gets tough.

- Have a clear sense of purpose in life.

- Clarify your goals and focus on them

- Be a risk taker. Step outside your comfort zone. Try something new.

- Polish your people skills.

- Hone your communications skills.

- Take excellent care of yourself.

- Positive expectations are the single, most outwardly identifiable, characteristics all successful people possess.

- Your reality is what you make it to be.

- You can train yourself to think more positively by training yourself to choose what you pay attention to and what you say about it, both to yourself and others. "We know what we are but know not what we may be." -Shakespeare.

- Whatever you believe, picture in your mind, and think about most of the time, you eventually will bring into reality.

- Your self-image is the most dominant factor that affects everything you attempt to do.

WORTHY QUOTES

"Assume a virtue, if you have it not." - Shakespeare.

"Act enthusiastic and you'll be enthusiastic." - Carnegie.

"Begin to be now what you will be hereafter." - St. Jerome.

"Repetition is the mother of skill."

"It is not the place, nor the condition, but the mind alone that can make any one happy or miserable." - L Estrange.

"Beliefs have the power to create and the power to destroy." -Robbins.

"Nothing is more likely to help a person overcome or endure troubles than the consciousness of having a task in life." -Frankl.

"The ancestor to every action is a thought." - Emerson.

"Imagination is more important than knowledge." -Albert Einstein.

"Things do not change; we change." -Thoreau.

"Change your thoughts and you change your world." -Norman Vincent Peale.

"Great men are those who see that thoughts rule the world." -Emerson.

"Nothing has any power over me other than that which I give it through my conscious thoughts." -Anthony Robbins.

"The greatest discovery of my generation is that human beings can alter their lives by altering their attitudes of mind." -William James.

"You are what you choose today." -Dyer.

"The only limits you have are the limits you believe." -Wayne Dyer.

"Anything we fail to reinforce will eventually dissipate." -Robbins.

"Patience is the companion of wisdom." -Augustine.

"The more he gives to others, the more he possesses of his own." -Lao-Tzu.

"What the mind can conceive and believe, it can achieve." -Hill.

"Believing is seeing." -Dyer.

"Customer relations is an integral part of your job-- not an extension of it." -William B. Martin, Quality Customer Service

"Customers perceive service in their own unique, idiosyncratic, emotional, irrational, end-of-the-day, and totally human terms. Perception is all there is!" - Tom Peters, Management guru

"Customer expectations of service organizations are loud and clear: look good, be responsive, be reassuring through courtesy and competence, be empathetic but, most of all, be reliable. Do what you said you would do. Keep the service promise." -Dr. Leonard Barry, Researcher, Texas A&M Un.

"Consistent, high-quality service boils down to two equally important things: caring and competence." - Chip R. Bell and Ron Zemke, Service Wisdom

"First impressions are the most lasting." -Proverb

"Use good judgment in all situations. There will be no additional rules." -Nordstrom, Inc., Employee Handbook.

"Politeness goes far, yet costs nothing." -Samuel Smiles, Nineteenth-century popular writer

"Gratitude is not only the greatest virtue but the mother of all the rest." -Cicero

(The above 8 quotations were taken from Delivering Knock Your Socks Off Service by Kristin Anderson and Ron Zemke--excellent book on customer service.)

Notice what has been repeated throughout these pages:

- Make the customer feel important.
- Be polite
- Be gracious
- Be attentive
- Listen
- Be positive
- Smile
- Be enthusiastic
- Be sincere
- Be nonjudgmental
- Be fair

And what have you done? You have made the customer feel important. If he/she feels that way, he/she will return to you again and again.

The payoff for you, the employee, is that you also will feel good, and feeling good is fun. Feeling good is positive, it's rewarding, so you too will feel important!

What is the quest of mankind--to feel good about themselves, to get satisfaction out of what they are doing--and guess what, you have just done that! Congratulations!

"Businesses often forget about the culture, and ultimately, they suffer for it because you can't deliver good service from unhappy employees."
- *Tony Hsieh, Founder of Zappos.com*

TEN WAYS TO ENHANCE YOUR CUSTOMER SERVICE

GOALS: Create community through the sharing of ideas, develop leadership, promote excellence, and prepare employees to the best of their abilities.

1. Give each employee a copy of The Secret Shopper Handbook.

2. Personalize the booklets with your company logo.

3. Have copies available for customers.

4. Include booklet in each new customer package.

5. Use for discussion with individual departments.

6. Encourage employees to use these concepts.

7. Ask employees to add to the lists.

8. Use individual lists as topics for general discussion. Find out where there is agreement and where there is not.

9. Use these principles as the basis for your company's standards.

10. Study the various lists and add new points and new topics. This will be an opportunity to expand the consciousness of employees and employers.

Don't find a fault; find a remedy.
-Henry Ford

EVALUATION OF OTHER BUSINESSES

The Secret Shopper

As part of a new employee's training, send each one to other similar businesses to make purchases and later return them.

Rate the effectiveness of the other business's employees according to the following:

10 = excellent to 0 = bad
0   5   10
"B" = before; "A" = after

   YOUR REACTIONS 10   5   0

"B"=before; "A"=after

1.   Time taken to recognize you   B   A
        B   A   B   A

2. Courtesy with which you were greeted   B   A
        0   5   10

3. Attitude of salesperson   B   A
        0   5   10

4. Helpfulness of salesperson   B   A
        0   5   10

5. Appearance of salesperson   B   A
        0   5   10

6. Sincerity of salesperson   B   A
        0   5   10

7. Condition of store compared with yours   B   A
        0   5   10

8. Listening ability of salesperson   B   A
        0   5   10

9. Satisfaction with transactions--purchase
    and refund   B   A
        0   5   10
10. Overall impression of buying and refunding
        experience:

11. What did you learn from this experience?

THE SECRET SHOPPER TRAINING

The Secret Shopper: This five-day, multiple format program for retail businesses consists of having sales personnel going into other businesses and using a checklist to evaluate sales personnel from other similar stores. Through this experiential method of learning, sales personnel can better understand the impact they have on customers each day.

This is a method is used in order to make employees feel special and, at the same time, instruct them in the basics of human nature, which translates into the "bottom line" for the employer.

POTENTIAL AUDIENCE: Retailers of every kind

In every town, in every city within the United States, there are retailers of some type--shoes, cameras, dresses, Housewares, food, etc.--and their livelihood depends on customers, preferably repeat customers. But do customers come back. If not, why?

An interesting study done many years ago concerning why people change their place of business may surprise you.

1%   died
3%   moved
4 & 7% had a relationship with someone in the company
9%   prices
14%   inferior merchandise
62%   ATTITUDE OF SOMEONE IN THE COMPANY

This is an amazing statistic! 62% of customers change their place of business because of how they were treated by someone in that store, someone who had a negative attitude.

Similar studies have been done in recent years, and essentially the same results are found. People place a high priority on how they are treated. How often have you been annoyed with an employee of a department store or retail store that you frequent? Bad attitude loses customers.

There are times, however, when an employee is not aware of how he or she is coming across to a customer. With this program, you have a tool to help that employee and all of their coworkers to have an experiential learning situation where they can find out for themselves what works and what does not work.

Obviously, employers want customers to return. Do their employees care? Store owners want their store to be known for service--are they? How many employers receive complaints about their customers?

A happy employee translates into a happy customer. First, however, the employee has to WANT to have a positive attitude. With this program, you can show them how.

The primary advantages of this program are:
•You can get customers happily returning to a store.
•You can develop satisfied employees
•You can help a retailer reap higher profits through satisfied customers who return again and again.
•You can help turn retail stores in more serene working environments.

The Secret Shopper 5-Day Teleclass Outline

AUDIENCE: Coaches who coach retailers or people working with the public

DAY ONE - Pretraining: Assessments for employees
1. Internal values
2. External values
3. Skills most enjoy using
4. Job positives and negatives
5. What you do naturally, effortlessly

DAY TWO
6. Philosophy
7. Attitude: Board of Trade Study, Swindoll essay, Logic, physiology
8. Nonverbal Communication
9. Verbal Communication
10. Human Relation Skills

DAY THREE

11. Listening
12. Perception
13. Understanding
14. Respectfulness
15. What is a customer?

DAY FOUR

16. 10 ways to appreciate customers
17. Customers: What they want from businesses
18. To help customers, businesses need to . . .
19. Tips for Employers
20. Tips for Employees

DAY FIVE - Assignment followup/evaluation

21. Review questions 1 - 5. What is impact on your attitude?
22. Review questions 6 - 10. What are your impressions about listening and body language?
23. Overall impression of buying and selling?
24. What did you learn from this experience?
25. What is most valuable thing you will take from this 5-day?

"High expectations are the key to everything." - Sam Walton, Founder of Wal-Mart

For more information on training, contact gail@coachability.com

www.ingramcontent.com/pod-product-compliance
Lightning Source LLC
Chambersburg PA
CBHW071545170526
45166CB00004B/1561

* 9 7 8 1 4 9 0 5 4 4 5 7 1 *